PRAISE FOR THE CLARITY FIELD GUIDE

Chris and Benj nailed it. This is a great how-to manual for helping a leader practice their most important discipline—taking a Clarity Break™.

—Gino Wickman
Author of *Traction* & *Entrepreneurial Leap*

The Clarity Field Guide completely demystifies the intimidating process of reflecting on your business. It provides a practical roadmap to "getting clear" with yourself and organized reflections tailored to the seasons of your life. Beware, procrastinators, Benj and Chris have destroyed any excuse against making clarity sessions a regular part of your week.

—Nicole Mennicke
Integrator™ & Vice President, Rocket Clicks

The Clarity Field Guide is a brilliant, fresh perspective on how to get really quiet within ourselves to define what matters most in our lives. Thoughtfully and creatively developed to bring out the best of purpose and passion in us all!

—Kelly Knight
Integrator™, EOS Worldwide

As a business owner or CEO, you are constantly fighting fires and moving from issue to issue. Without taking a moment (or several) to sit back and work "on" your business, you will continue to spin your wheels. Chris and Benj show us how it's possible to leave the grind and gain perspective for the long-term health of your business which is ultimately the most important opportunity to address. Thankful to have them on our team!

—Tyler Dolph
Visionary & President
Rocket Clicks

If you ever wished that being an entrepreneur came with a book of answers, here it is! Spoiler alert: The answers are inside of you! Chris and Benj have just dared to ask the brilliant questions. What will your story be?

—Jill Young
Author of The Advantage Series
& Certified EOS Implementer®

Chris and Benj take us out of the "rat race" with the enormous power of beautiful questions. These questions ground us and move us back to the bigger picture so we as leaders can focus on the greater game we were put here to play.

—Lieutenant Colonel (Retired) Scott Mann
Green Beret & Founder of Rooftop Leadership

I have been following the teachings of Benj Miller and Chris White for years to maximize not only organizational potential, but also to turbocharge my own personal path. I am thankful to the both of them for their insightful contributions to the leadership knowledge bank.

—John Amtmann, EdD (Educational Leadership)
Professor of Kinesiology, Montana Tech

If reflective thinking in your business feels impossible with your schedule, if it's not really your style, or it doesn't feel "productive," then this is your solution. Chris and Benj give leaders a focused method for answering the most important questions we can ask about ourselves and our business. It will challenge your thinking and clarify what you need to do in your specific season as a leader.

—Clay Scroggins
Lead Pastor, Buckhead Church

The Clarity Field Guide is a great reminder for quick-start Visionaries to focus on the Planning Season. Chris and Benj remind us to slow down, resist the "ready, fire, aim" approach, and instead lean into the energy to create a solid plan to move our businesses forward.

—Alec Broadfoot
Visionary, VisionSpark

As an avid believer of clarity breaks, there is no doubt of their impact on me professionally and my companies. However, I have sometimes wondered if I am asking myself the RIGHT questions at the RIGHT time. Benj and Chris provide clarity on thought-provoking questions to ask yourself for the right season. I will bring *The Clarity Field Guide* to every Clarity Break™ from now on to remind myself of the key points and ensure I am getting the most out of my clarity break by asking the right questions at the right time.

—Kristic Clayton
Integrator™ for BCR Wealth
& Visionary/Integrator for Female Integrator Mastermind (FIM)

Through this guide, Chris and Benj show business leaders how it's possible to leave the grind and gain perspective for the current season. It's been an incredibly transformative tool for me as a business owner

—Emily Morgan
Founder & CEO
Delegate Solutions

I love *The Clarity Field Guide!* It's helped me keep things simple in a world that seems to be growing ever more complex. Chris and Benj did a fantastic job giving us a path to follow to help solve our most significant issues. This guide has helped me rise above our organization and work on it, not in it. It's a must for anyone looking to grow personally or professionally.

—Casey Cavell
Integrator™ for Rocket Fuel & Advisor

You need to go here. Enter into the danger of the questions. On the other side you will find breakthrough for yourself and your organization.

—Dr. Benjamin Hardy, PhD
Best Selling Author & Organizational Psychologist

THE CLARITY FIELD GUIDE

THE CLARITY FIELD GUIDE

the answers no one else can give you

Benj Miller & Chris White

ethos collective

Printed in the United States of America

Published by **ethos collective**™
PO Box 43, Powell, OH 43065
ethoscollective.vip

LCCN: 2020919941
ISBN: 978-1-63680-003-5 (paperback)
ISBN: 978-1-63680-004-2 (hardback)
ISBN: 978-1-63680-005-9 (ebook)

With Gratitude

To our wonderful wives, **Erica Miller** and **Darlene White**. Thank you for the ways that you push us to be our best and love us through our worst.

To **McKenzie Reeves Decker**, you made this book actually happen. Thank you for helping us capture the chaos of our minds.

To **John Richie**, you have inspired our lives and the content of this book. May you be blessed from the ripples of your life.

If I was to sum up the single biggest mistake of senior leadership in the Information Age, it's a lack of reflection. Solitude allows you to reflect while others are reacting. We need solitude to refocus on prospective decision-making, rather than just reacting to problems as they arise.

—James Mattis
4-star Marine Corps General
& Former Secretary of Defense

CONTENTS

SURVEYING THE LAND

We grew up in the Midwest (Chris in Illinois and Benj in Ohio) in and around typical farming communities—known for fertile land, cattle, and corn for miles. Neither of us stayed in those places. Benj moved to Atlanta to start his businesses amid asphalt, traffic-stacked streets, the arts, culture, and creative energy. Chris moved to Orlando, Florida, with its white beaches, wide-spanning communities, and booming business opportunities.

Occasionally, we talk about what it was like many years ago in our small towns. We both loved growing up there. For places that were—to the naked eye—fairly standard, it was special to both of us in the way it shaped our thinking and how we run our businesses today. Strangely enough, maybe one of the most profound, proud symbols we carry with us from our lives in the Midwest is the farmer's mentality. Seriously. But we're talking about more than denim overalls, mud-caked work boots, tattered ball caps, weathered hands, a permanent tan line on the back of the neck, and gritty nails. We're talking about their rhythm, their culture, their tie to the land.

We both believe the people who worked the land in our towns were, and still are, great American heroes. We watched these men and women work every day, in every season, with their hands in the dirt and dust in their hair, bringing life from hundreds of acres of land by planting, harvesting, replanting, and waiting for the crops to rise again. These farmers brought in thousands of workers every season for harvesting. They gave many jobs to countless people in our towns and fed families nearby and in surrounding states. They are the foundation of enterprise.

As boys who later grew up to be successful entrepreneurs, our first impression of the grit, consistency, and trust in the process we witnessed in the farming community became the cornerstone for how we think about our work. Who knew, after all this time, we would both carry this symbol of a great work ethic through the start-ups we founded and businesses we run? It was shocking to us that something so common, trivial, and in the background created such a simple and logical model for how we should work and live.

We intentionally start with these memories of our farming communities because they represent the same spirit in all of us. Every person stakes and sows their own plots in business, real estate, healthcare, really any job or industry. There is something noble and respectable about a hard-laboring person like a farmer. And it's forged our beliefs about work ethic and responsibility, but the more we talk about it, it holds something even more than that.

Yes, the farmer acts, moves, pushes, pulls, harnesses, and leads. But the farmer also surveys. She knows her land, plots her tracts, walks the fields, and stands back to see it fully. The survey—the moment of perspective and total vision—is the purpose of this book. As a farmer of your own "fields," you do not need another manual to operate the tractor or advice on how to yield the best crop. You have that and lose sleep over it already. This is a guide to gaining clarity in your life and business. You'll do it by standing still and surveying yourself so you can have a clear vision of the great work ahead.

GAINING VISION

As entrepreneurs with over forty combined years of experience in start-ups, corporations, and consulting, we are now leveraging what we have learned—both good and bad—to coach and train diverse companies through the System & Soul Framework™. It's a business operating framework we have seen help teams of businesses leaders avoid pitfalls while accelerating results. The transformation and breakthrough we see in our work is truly amazing!

However, our clients seem to miss one thing that absolutely kills them. Some call it taking a Clarity Break™; Michael Hyatt calls it Full Focus; Franklin Covey has a day-planner system for it; and Rachel Hollis calls it her Start Today journal, but they all come down to the same discipline: focused thinking and reflection. The goal of each system is to create a habit, but if you ask us or look at the blank pages in all our journals, you'd see we struggle to make time, do the work, and follow the system. We hear the same thing from our clients too. It seems there is too much to track and at the same time, not enough "meat" in these systems to satisfy.

The difficulty most of us have with this habit doesn't change the fact that every successful leader, entrepreneur, and visionary we have ever known or heard about uses focused thinking and reflection. Marcus Aurelius did it to lead the Roman Empire; Steve Jobs did it to change telecommunications forever; and Oprah Winfrey did it to create a major media conglomerate. The examples are endless; the success is unprecedented, and we tell our clients about these stories of leaders who take time to get clarity. And yet here we are, treating it like flossing!

As visionaries and innovators, we saw this tension as an opportunity to solve a problem with which we all struggle. So, that is how we got here. We have seen ourselves and business owner after business owner ignore their personal and organizational need to get away and gain perspective on the current moment. Then, you know what happens? We see people managing stress, making impulsive decisions, quitting, perpetuating flash-in-the-pan business ideas, leaving jobs at a high turnover rate, and eventually burning out. The excuses are always the same: "I don't have time;" "I'm not a writer;" and "I have so much in my head; I wouldn't even know where to start." There are always going to be barriers if you are seeking them. But if you are looking for barriers, you are victimizing yourself.

Visionaries (and we all have the capacity and potential to be visionaries) see a preferred future and create a path to it. They make change happen—*transformational* change. With transformational change, your head and heart connect to a greater purpose. Everything you do then becomes an act of flow instead of force. You look out onto your tract of land with a sense of direction like you have never experienced. You have this in you. It's just a choice you must make.

Part of what we see in the clients we lead through this process is a lack of awareness about themselves. They do not know how they think, feel, why they react, or what they believe at the core of their being. They're baffled by what sounds simple and straightforward but is one of the hardest questions to answer: "What do I want?" This is not some weird yogi, meditative "empty your mind" stuff we are talking about; it's a matter of human capacity. The leader's emotional health and awareness determine his capacity. If your beliefs and decisions come from an insecure place or void in your life, it will radiate through your organization. The best thing you can do is take this time for yourself and your company to bring your best to the workplace.

Our desire is for you to live your life with full freedom, meaning you are

- doing what you love with people you love
- creating something with meaning, purpose, and value (full impact)
- enjoying your life and the people outside your work.

You already know this: you are a busy leader and could occupy your time all day, every day with challenges and opportunities. You probably already are. Unfortunately, that grind does not mean you end up finding full freedom.

What you may not know is this: the way you think throughout your creative and working life can either lead you to or pull you further away from full freedom. You may not be totally aware of how your thoughts are affecting your beliefs and the actions you take in your business. It isn't a fault; it's a reality. As human beings, we have natural wiring that urges us to act for survival and protection. We are also conditioned over our lifetimes by circumstances that contribute to us being guarded, ambitious, anxious, hyperactive, or perhaps boldly independent. Those attributes are probably some reasons why you are so profoundly good at what you do, but they are also the things that keep you on the hamster wheel. The hamster wheel will work your muscles and wear you out but will get you nowhere. Our system will help you clear the path, remove barriers, open the view, and put meat on the bone of what it means to break away and gain clearer vision.

KEEP IT SIMPLE

We want to make gaining clarity simple and directed. No crazy, complicated processes. No fluffy questions. Just the things that have helped us and the leaders we know drive breakthrough thinking and remarkable results. This book contains nearly 100 of the most impactful, clarifying questions we could find to help you experience intentional, clear thinking. These questions over our forty-plus years of experience have led us out of poor business decisions, developed powerful teams, saved us time, money and our asses, and helped us to elevate the right people to the right seats. The practice of gaining clarity through these questions will help you protect your confidence and intuition, get away from negative influences, and talk to yourself about your business. We designed these questions to encourage you to think about things you have not considered or have ignored. They are here to bring your best thoughts out of your head and onto the paper and help you develop awareness.

Here are key things to remember through this process:

- **You will not stumble across free time for this depth of thinking and reflection.** It should be planned and blocked in your calendar. Unless you give it priority, it will be easy to drop to the bottom of your to-do list.

- **You will not be good at this the first time, and you may wander.** That's okay. Keep working the muscle. The habit will get stronger, your insights will become more profound, and your vision will be clearer.
- **It is hard to gain clarity when you worry about doing it "right."** Perfection is not a friend here. Allow yourself to work with partial ideas and lingering questions. If you could figure it all out and do it perfectly the first time, you would be superhuman. Don't put that pressure on yourself.
- **Not every question is the right question for your current season.** Not every season is the right season to make certain decisions. We have categorized the questions in this book by the four seasons of life that we adapted from our friend, mentor, and executive coach, John Richie. We call it the Creator's Cycle. We believe you will be most successful using this model to understand and lean into the season you are in.
- **The objective is to use this book for over a year.** If you can plan ahead, book your clarity sessions on a bi-weekly or monthly basis. We recommend ninety minutes or more for these sessions.
- **Stick with one or two questions in a clarity session.** The intention of these questions is to make you think long and hard. So, find

one or two questions that scare you, challenge you, or you avoid, then dig in there for the time you have.

The next section of this book will describe the four seasons in the Creator's Cycle. Then, you'll take an assessment to define your current season. It will act as a guide to leverage the reflection questions in the appropriate section. We believe this process and the thoughtful time you give to it can transform your day-to-day as a business leader and as a hard-working, purpose-driven person. But it starts with a willingness. It starts with you. You are here to gain clarity.

Best of luck,
Benj and Chris

THE CREATOR'S CYCLE

Here's what we know to be true: regardless of circumstance or ability, we all move through seasons of life. Think about it.

Week by week, month by month, even year by year, you can look back and categorize the "season" you were in emotionally, mentally, or physically. Some seasons were about planning the future and setting goals. Some seasons were nose-to-the-grindstone, executing, growing, and going. In other seasons, you felt lethargic, dispassionate, and frustrated. Then, you regained a sense of excitement for life, a dream for the future, and remembered your purpose.

The seasons we just described are pervasive in the human experience and documented in psychological research as the stages of the life cycle: birth, adolescence, adulthood, and old age. We see this in business, too, in the stages of the product and business cycles: introduction, growth, maturity, decline/recovery. We see it most in nature: spring, summer, autumn, and winter.

As you use this book, you will benefit from being aware of your current season. Not every question or train of thought will benefit you in the current moment. Not every season is the right season to make the decisions you are considering. These seasons will teach you your rhythms. The questions will show you how to sit in them with gratitude and a higher level of awareness. The time and thought you put in will lead you to greater insights.

The four seasons are: Planning (Spring), Executing (Summer), The Doldrums (Autumn), and Cocooning (Winter). We will use the four seasons and that great picture of the farmer we mentioned earlier as an analogy to explain how a person moves through these seasons emotionally and in their work life as a leader and entrepreneur.

Let's unpack the seasons of the Creator's Cycle more. Once you are familiar with the concept, you can take the Creator's Cycle Assessment on the following pages.

1. PLANNING

You're in the idea season, writing and mapping the plans for the next phase of your life. You feel optimistic, confident, and creative. New ideas are fuel, everything is an opportunity, and you are searching for the best next thing and how to go after it.

Results from the Planning Season:

- High energy
- Lots of ideas
- Clarifying identity
- Increasing confidence
- Defining what's important
- Renewing close relationships
- More creativity
- More risk-taking

2. EXECUTING

This is the most positive, visible, and powerful part of the Cycle. You are living your dream and working your plan. This season of life is accomplishment oriented. You're maintaining habits, excitement is headed toward a plateau, and you could be well on your way to coasting. In this season, you feel secure, energized, full of momentum, and purposeful. You are content but still driven to keep building and following the patterns you have established.

Results from the Executing Season:

- Extreme focus
- Ability to produce quantity and quality of work
- Reaching goals
- Expanding goals
- Advancement
- Securing financial rewards
- Fulfillment
- Using unique abilities
- Delegating and elevating others
- Following your sense of purpose

3. THE DOLDRUMS

You've arrived at a downtime, even though you appear to be on top of the world. Why? Because you are a builder and a doer. In this season, your plans are either humming along or are not quite as fulfilling as you had hoped. Success is boring, and failure is demoralizing. You feel a private pessimism growing. Your motivation wanes. Your dreams go away or no longer excite you. You feel trapped. Maybe you even feel like a victim.

Results from The Doldrums Season:

- Depression or crisis

- Re-questioning life, identity, purpose
- Lack of energy
- Distracted by life's false promises of happiness

4. COCOONING

This season is both at the end and beginning of the Creator's Cycle. This part of the Cycle is fertile ground for the germination of new ideas. The transition to the Planning season starts in the cocoon, so keep in mind how important this season is as you grow into the next iteration of your life and business.

Take a timeout and move away from the limelight. Shift your focus inward for healing, reflection, and discovery. Clean up and clean out. Build on what you learned, press into who you really are, and ponder whether you want the same things as the last time you went through this season. Finally, you will emerge with the birth of a new purpose.

Results from the Cocooning Season:

- Sabbatical agenda
- Personal growth
- Spiritual renewal
- Inner peace
- Solitude
- Personal confidence

As you answer the questions specifically chosen for each season, you will be astounded by the insights you gain and how they can correct your course.

Our advice as you begin is to be gracious to yourself. Stay in your thoughts as long as you can and listen. You'll discover that providing room for perspective to unfold is one of the most rewarding things you can do in your entire work life.

Take the Creator's Cycle Assessment on the next page to get started.

THE CREATOR'S CYCLE ASSESSMENT

Start by answering these questions, then find the section of this book that best fits where you are today. Keep in mind—you may pass through the seasons of the Creator's Cycle several times in a month, season, or year. Where you are and how often you pass through these seasons is individual to you. It says nothing about your ability to lead or lead well; it only serves as a vulnerable starting place to ask yourself the questions that matter most.

How am I feeling?

Creative and thoughtful.

If I could spend my time doing one thing it would be...

Learning about myself, dreaming, evaluating experiences.

Inventing, planning next steps, aspiring toward a bigger vision.

Like quitting.

THE DOLDRUMS

Busy.

And...

distracted. Like there's something else I'd rather be doing.

hustling. I've got a lot to do, but I'm energized.

And if I could do anything it would be...	Answer... Is this what I want? Am I fulfilled? Why not?	**C**
	Answer... How my idea can work?	**P**
My biggest challenge right now is...	getting a game plan and strategizing how to do it.	**P**
	identifying the right people and processes.	**E**
And what I want most of all is...	time to think and process. the last season.	**C**
	a nap...I'm missing energy, engagement, and challenge.	**D**
But it feels like something is missing...	A solid plan and measurable goals.	**P**
	"polish" to our processes, alignment, growth.	**E**

C=COCOONING D=THE DOLDRUMS E=EXECUTING P=PLANNING

TIPS ON HOW TO USE THIS BOOK:

- Schedule time in your calendar to work with this book. We recommend a minimum of ninety minutes per clarity session.
- Find a quiet space where you cannot be interrupted.
- Bring ONLY this book and something to write with.
- **Review the Creator's Cycle Assessment every time you begin a clarity session.**
- The allegory at the beginning of each session is intended to help dial in your thoughts and provide a context for each season. Read them and meditate on the words and ideas before you jump into the questions. Quotes are also paired with each question to provide you the wisdom or perspective of some of the most successful minds in and before our time.
- **Within the season you choose, find one or two questions to focus on in the time you have.** We recommend focusing on the questions you are drawn to or fear. They will probably lead you to profound insight or impart wisdom into key areas you need to consider.
- Take notes as you go. We've designed this book to give you space to engage with the questions. By taking notes, you will solidify

thoughts and create a journal to revisit your previous thoughts and gauge your progress.

- Take your time. Don't rush your thinking or expect brilliant strokes of insight, genius, or epiphanies.
- Take a deep breath. Give your thoughts space.
- Get clear.

SPRING: PLANNING

THE PLANNING SEASON

The soil is tilled. The mornings are crisp but give way to warm afternoons, strong winds, and days of light rain. This is the season of anticipation and optimism. All the elements are there, and life is intensifying powerfully toward the surface. In your work and the work of the farmer, there is room here to plant your dreams. The time spent inside, thinking about the opportunity in the frozen ground this winter, leads you to draw up plans for your land, map your plots, and look for new ways to make this year's harvest even stronger, yield more, and generate greater demand.

You are in the idea season. As the days get longer and brighter, you have every reason to feel optimistic, confident, and creative. Your energy feels boundless, and you are grateful to stretch your legs, walk your fields, survey, take notes, and press seeds to soil. The energy in you is surging for the clear opportunity to take root.

DO:

- Ask, "How are we going to do it? How do we make it happen?"
- Focus your vision and map it out.
- Lean into the energy you possess to create a solid plan.

DON'T:

- Execute as you develop the plan.
- Chase shiny objects.
- Rush to get started; avoid a ready, fire, aim scenario.

What is the most important idea to ponder today?

Nurture your mind with great thoughts, for you will never go any higher than you think.

—Benjamin Disraeli
Former Prime Minister to the United Kingdom

How can I change my perspective?

Pain, discomfort, shock, boredom, impostor syndrome, awkwardness, fear, being wrong, failing, ignorance, looking stupid: Your avoidance of these feelings is stopping you from a life greater than your wildest imagination. These are the feelings that accompany a life of success. And yet, these are the very feelings most often avoided. They are avoided because, as stated previously, most people have developed an extreme avoidance orientation toward life.

—Dr. Benjamin Hardy, PhD
Organizational Psychologist & Bestselling Author

What does success look like for me?

Would you like me to give you a formula for success? It's quite simple, really: Double your rate of failure. You are thinking of failure as the enemy of success. But it isn't at all. You can be discouraged by failure or you can learn from it, so go ahead and make mistakes. Make all you can. Because remember that's where you'll find success.

—Thomas J. Watson
Former Chairman & CEO, IBM

What is on my bucket list?

The man who has no imagination has no wings.

—Muhammad Ali

What does my dream workday look like? Could I make that every day?

Do not lose hold of your dreams or aspirations. For if you do, you may still exist, but you have ceased to live.

—Henry David Thoreau

If a recession comes in the next three years, what will I wish I had done now?

In reality strategy is actually very straightforward. You pick a general direction and implement like hell.

—Jack Welch
Former Chairman & CEO, General Electric

What are the important risks our company faces, and what should I do about them?

If you're prepared and you know what it takes, it's not a risk. You just have to figure out how to get there. There is always a way to get there.

—Mark Cuban
Entrepreneur & Investor

What do I fear being asked?

It takes humility to realize we don't know everything, not to rest on our laurels, and to know that we must keep learning and observing. If we don't, we can be sure some startup will be there to take our place.

—Cher Wang
Founder, HTC & VIA Technologies

In what ways is my business unable to grow beyond me? What should I do about that?

If your dream only includes you, it's too small.

—Ava DuVernay
Filmmaker

Am I giving all areas of my life appropriate energy?

Your work is going to fill a large part of your life, and the only way to be truly satisfied is to do what you believe is great work. And the only way to do great work is to love what you do.

—Steve Jobs
Co-Founder, Apple Computers

Where is my soul in this decision?

A soul without a center feels constantly vulnerable to people or circumstances. Your soul is what integrates your will (your intentions), your mind (your thoughts and feelings, your values and conscience), and your body (your face, body language, and actions) into a single life. A soul is healthy—well-ordered—when there is harmony between these three entities and God's intent for all creation. When you are connected with God and other people in life, you have a healthy soul.

—John Ortberg
Pastor & Author

Is there a third option for the decision I am facing?

We are not interested in the possibilities of defeat; they do not exist.

—Queen Victoria

What should I delegate?

The best executive is the one who has sense enough to pick good men to do what he wants done, and self-restraint to keep from meddling while they do it.

—Theodore Roosevelt

Are there ways I am compromising my own standards?

The "with God" life is not a life of more religious activities or devotions or trying to be good. It is a life of inner peace and contentment for your soul with the maker and manager of the universe. The "without God" life is the opposite. It is death. It will kill your soul.

—John Ortberg
Pastor & Author

Am I leading my family as intentionally as my business?

I'm convinced that the man who has learned to meditate upon the Lord will be able to run on his feet and walk in his spirit. Although he may be hurried by his vocation, that's not the issue. The issue is how fast his spirit is going. To slow it down takes a period of time.

—Charles Stanley
Pastor & Author

What would we need to do to get our three-year plan done in half the time?

As an entrepreneur, if you're the originator, you need to be faster than ever.

—Niklaus Zennstrom
Co-Founder, Skype

What issues or struggles are preventing me from getting what I want from the business?

I can't change the direction of the wind, but I can adjust my sails to always reach my destination.

—Jimmy Dean
Founder, Jimmy Dean, Actor & Musician

What are my expectations of the people around me? What do they expect from me?

We rise by lifting others.

—Robert Ingersoll
Writer & Speaker

What are the relationships I need to invest in?

None of us is as smart as all of us.

—Ken Blanchard
Author & Speaker

What market conditions make us vulnerable?

There is only one boss: the customer. And he can fire everybody in the company, from the chairman on down, simply by spending his money somewhere else.

—Sam Walton
Founder, Walmart & Sam's Club

What are the five lessons I most need to learn?

By three methods we may learn wisdom: First, by reflection, which is noblest; Second, by imitation, which is easiest; and third by experience, which is the bitterest.

—Confucius

What is my plan?

A woodsman was once asked, "What would you do if you had just five minutes to chop down a tree?" He answered, "I would spend the first two and a half minutes sharpening my axe."

—Anonymous

What should I stop doing?

We think mistakenly that success is the result of the amount of time we put in at work, instead of the quality of time we put in.

—Arianna Huffington
Founder, Huffington Post

What should I do more of?

Only the best is good enough.

—Ole Kirk Christiansen
Founder, The Lego Group

SUMMER: EXECUTING

THE EXECUTING SEASON

You ring the bell and call the farm hands together. Work needs to be done: fields must be watered, fences must be mended, and rows need weeding. The list is long, but you are not alone to tend to your dream.

In deep summer, you are bent over, back to the sun alongside the willing workers who help you maintain and foster the growth in the fields you planted. You are working hard. But you breathe easy seeing your ideas and plans come together and explode into a true reality.

This is the most positive season in the Creator's Cycle. You are living your dream and working your plan. This season of life is accomplishment oriented. As you maintain habits, excitement plateaus, and you could begin to coast. In this phase, you feel secure, energized, full of momentum, and purposeful. It's time to enjoy and refine what you brought to life.

DO:

- Align your resources: people, talent, and materials.
- Bring the vision to the ground and begin the work.
- Clarify roles.
- Orchestrate and communicate with the team to keep them on track with the vision.

DON'T:

- Coast on your initial success; stay motivated.
- Try to do it all on your own; delegate and elevate.
- Get distracted by other opportunities outside your vision.

Am I giving all areas of my life appropriate energy?

There is virtue in work and there is virtue in rest. Use both and overlook neither.

—Alan Cohen
Author

How can I change my perspective?

A lot of people in our industry haven't had very diverse experiences. So, they don't have enough dots to connect, and they end up with very linear solutions without a broad perspective on the problem. The broader one's understanding of the human experience, the better design we will have.

—Steve Jobs
Co-Founder, Apple Computers

What decisions must we make?

I learned to always take on things I'd never done before. Growth and comfort do not coexist.

—Ginni Rometty
Former Chairman, President & CEO, IBM

What should I delegate?

Are we limiting our success by not mastering the art of delegation?... it's simply a matter of preparation meeting opportunity.

—Oprah Winfrey

What should we simplify?

The secret of success is to do the common thing uncommonly well.

—John D. Rockefeller Jr.
Financier & Philanthropist

Which business activities are not leading us toward our vision and mission?

Opportunity lies in the place where the complaints are.

—Jack Ma
Founder, Alibaba

How should I leverage the success or power I hold?

He who wishes to be obeyed must know how to command.

—Niccolò Machiavelli

What is most important for me to ponder today?

Either you run the day or the day runs you.

—Jim Rohn
Author & Speaker

Am I focusing on the most important things?

Fight for the things that you care about but do it in a way that will lead others to you.

—Ruth Bader Ginsburg
Former Supreme Court Justice

What have I neglected?

I think failure is nothing more than life's way of nudging you that you are off course. My attitude to failure is not attached to outcome, but in not trying. It is liberating. Most people attach failure to something not working out or how people perceive you. This way, it is about answering to yourself.

—Sara Blakely
Founder, Spanx

What do I fear being asked?

You gain strength, courage, and confidence by every experience in which you really stop to look fear in the face. You are able to say to yourself, 'I have lived through this horror. I can take the next thing that comes along.' You must do the thing you think you cannot do.

—Eleanor Roosevelt

How can we be more proactive?

If opportunity doesn't knock, build a door.

—Milton Berle
Actor & Comedian

What do our customers think about our product or service?

You can market your ass off, but if your product sucks, you're dead.

—Gary Vaynerchuk
Bestselling Author & Speaker

Who do I mistrust and why? Is there something I should do about it?

Trust, but verify.

—Ronald Reagan

What is my top priority this week? This month?

Lack of direction, not lack of time, is the problem. We all have twenty-four-hour days.

—Zig Ziglar
Author & Speaker

Is the vision and plan for the business or department on track? What is the number one goal?

Good order is the foundation of all things.

—Edmund Burke
Statesman & Philosopher

Do I understand what my direct reports love to do and do well? Am I leveraging their strengths?

People do not care how much you know until they know how much you care.

—John C. Maxwell
Bestselling Author & Speaker

Who would be devastating to lose (hit-by-a-bus scenario)? What should I do about that?

Dollars have never been known to produce character, and character will never be produced by money. I'll invest my money in people.

—W.K. Kellogg
Founder, The Kellogg Company

If I lose a key player, do I have someone ready to fill the seat? Are my processes working well?

The strength of the team is each individual member. The strength of each member is the team.

—Phil Jackson
Eleven NBA Championships (Coach)
& Two NBA Championships (Player)

What personnel move must I make soon? How strong is my bench?

Your job as leader is to stay as close in touch as possible with those closest to the action.

—Kat Cole
CEO, Focus Brands

What are the priorities and goals of those closest to me?

As we look ahead into the next century, leaders will be those who empower others.

—Bill Gates
Founder, Microsoft

What issues or struggles are preventing me from getting what I want from the business?

But until a person can say deeply and honestly, "I am what I am today because of the choices I made yesterday," that person cannot say, "I choose otherwise."

—Stephen R. Covey
Author & Speaker

How can I improve communication?

Vulnerability is not winning or losing; it's having the courage to show up and be seen when we have no control over the outcome.

—Brene Brown
Professor, Researcher, & Author

Do I have the right people in the right seats to grow?

Motivation comes from working on things we care about. It also comes from working with people we care about.

—Sheryl Sandberg
COO, Facebook

Whom should I be elevating?

The greatest asset of a company is its people.

—Jorge Paulo Lemann
Co-founder, Banco Garantia

How is my business unable to grow beyond me? What should I do about that?

A leader has the vision and conviction that a dream can be achieved. He inspires the power and energy to get it done.

—Ralph Lauren
Fashion Designer

AUTUMN: THE DOLDRUMS

THE DOLDRUMS

You look out just as an early dusk settles and watch your field workers harvest the crop. Dry ground, baled hay, and a cold cutting wind are the only things left behind as they move over the land.

What now?

There is plenty to be grateful for and celebrate. You can see the success of the work you envisioned and sweated over all summer. But there is a shadow coming over you. You know this feeling. It's like disappointment, lethargy, boredom, or worse—depression. Something is wrong here. And the feeling makes you think you would like nothing more than to wander off for a while, forget your land, forget your team, forget the usual hum of preparations you must begin for the next season, and just find a new plot.

In the Creator's Cycle, both success and failure lead to the same end: The Doldrums. You think more and more about what else is out there. Maybe this dream is not what you thought it would be, and you are tired of it. The dream is as dried out as the soil it was planted in.

Resist falling down the slope of self-criticism here. It will only lead you to darker, less clear places in this season. Go inside. Let yourself lean into the sorrow at the end of the summer. Now is the time to watch the leaves fall away and look inward at the person, the process, and the pain of the work. Now is the time to remember there is understanding and beauty in the downfall. The success of your dream is not a straight line. The fields will not stay green forever; they cannot, and neither can you. Lean into the dimness inside you.

DO:

- Recognize the season for what it is and lean in.
- Ask yourself what you are feeling and where those feelings might be rooted.
- Take space from your work, step back if you can, and make room.
- Review your vision and stay the course as best you can.
- Remember that success is not a straight line.

DON'T:

- Ignore your feeling of "burnout."
- Allow your negative thoughts and self-criticism to take over and send you spiraling.
- Try to push through and bury your head in more work to avoid these hard feelings.
- Get distracted by "greener pastures."
- Give up yet.

Why is this season/challenge/feeling still happening?

We are not made for the mountains, for sunrises, or for the other beautiful attractions in life—those are simply intended to be moments of inspiration. We are made for the valley and the ordinary things of life and that is where we have to prove our stamina and strength.

—Oswald Chambers
Evangelist & Teacher

Am I giving all areas of my life appropriate energy?

We need to do a better job of putting ourselves higher on our to-do list.

—Michelle Obama

Which business activities are not leading toward our vision and mission?

Building a mission and building a business go hand in hand.

—Mark Zuckerburg
Founder, Facebook

What are the most profitable decisions I have made in the last three years?

Longevity in this business is about being able to reinvent yourself or invent the future.

—Satya Nadella
CEO, Microsoft

What fulfills me?

Your long-term happiness and fulfillment depend on your ability to fulfill your soul's unique purpose and to fill the place in the world that only you can fill, making the contribution that only you can make.

—Rod Stryker
Author & Teacher

What hard things am I avoiding?

...feelings like disappointment, embarrassment, irritation, resentment, anger, jealousy, and fear, instead of being bad news, are actually very clear moments that teach us where it is that we're holding back. They teach us to perk up and lean in when we feel we'd rather collapse and back away. They're like messengers that show us, with terrifying clarity, exactly where we're stuck. This very moment is the perfect teacher and lucky for us, it's with us wherever we are.

—Pema Chödrön
Buddhist Nun

Am I giving all areas of my life appropriate energy?

The difference between successful people and really successful people is that really successful people say no to almost everything.

—Warren Buffett
CEO, Berkshire Hathaway

In what ways am I lonely?

Yet it is in this loneliness that the deepest activities begin. It is here that you discover act without motion, labor that is profound repose, vision in obscurity, and, beyond all desire, a fulfillment whose limits extend to infinity.

—Thomas Merton
Trappist Monk

How is my business unable to grow beyond me? What should I do about that?

The empires of the future are empires of the mind.

—Winston Churchill

What should I delegate?

The really expert riders of horses let the horse know immediately who is in control, but then guide the horse with loose reins and seldom use the spurs.

—Sandra Day O'Connor
Former Supreme Court Justice

What lies am I believing?

Shame is a soul eating emotion.

—Carl Gustav Jung

How can I change my perspective?

No problem can be solved from the same level of consciousness that created it.

—Albert Einstein

What might my Higher Power be saying to me?

It is much more important to cultivate the quiet, inward space of a constant listening than to always be approaching God for a specific direction. Faith is not opposed to knowledge; faith is opposed to sight. And grace is not opposed to effort; it is opposed to earning.

—Dallas Willard

What do I fear being asked?

Avoiding danger is no safer in the long run than outright exposure. The fearful are caught as often as the bold.

—Helen Keller

Who would my coworkers say I am? What would my children, spouse, and investors say?

One lives in the hope of becoming a memory.

—Antonio Porchia
Poet

How have I given people reason to mistrust me?

The day soldiers stop bringing you their problems is the day you have stopped leading them. They have either lost confidence that you can help them or concluded that you do not care. Either case is a failure of leadership.

—General Colin Powell

Is my spiritual life strong enough to withstand a storm?

If we do not create and control our environment, our environment creates and controls us.

—Dr. Marshall Goldsmith
Executive Leadership Coach

What is the most important thing for me to ponder today?

Change your thoughts and you can change your world.

—Norman Vincent Peale

What issues or struggles are keeping me from getting what I want from the business?

Every person takes the limits of their own field of vision for the limits of the world.

—Arthur Schopenhauer

In what ways is my business unable to grow beyond me? What should I do about that?

Letting go and trusting others to do things well is one of the more challenging aspects of being a leader of a growing organization.

—Verne Harnish
Author & Speaker

WINTER: COCOONING

THE COCOONING SEASON

While the fields are fallow and your storerooms are full, you make peace with the pull between activity and attending to yourself. This is where you look at your own hands—the new blisters and scars. You look at their strength when you curl your fingers in, and you think about the power in you to do the work you were designed for. There is peace in this season, gratitude, and the slow come-and-go of reflective thoughts on the past months of triumph and toil. You accomplished so much. It was not perfect; maybe it was nothing like you expected. But the challenge has shaped you, made you different and better. You are unfolding revelations learned from that hardship every day.

You are paying attention and letting the focus on your past and dreams be a catalyst for what is coming.

DO:

- Find solitude.
- Engage in new thought patterns and ideas.
- Contemplate and create. Reflect on the past.
- Dream about the future.

DON'T:

- Jump into anything new too quickly without letting the idea germinate.
- Fill your time until you don't have enough time to think and create.
- Avoid looking at past failures; they are our greatest teachers.
- Get stuck in the past and forget the future.

What does my dream workday look like? Could I make that every day?

Nothing is really work unless you would rather be doing something else.

—J.M. Barrie
Novelist

What is my mission?

Without a mission statement, you may get to the top of the ladder and then realize it was leaning against the wrong building.

—Dave Ramsey
Founder, Ramsey Solutions

If another CEO took over my business, what would she change and why?

In sports and in business, the greatest leaders are those who make the best decisions in the most crucial of situations. They are the ones who focus their energy on turning tough decisions into winning decisions.

—Don Yaeger
Bestselling Author & Speaker

How should I handle the success or power I hold?

Leadership is not about titles, positions or flowcharts. It is about one life influencing another.

—John C. Maxwell
Bestselling Author & Speaker

How could I create more value for my customers?

My definition of innovative, is providing value to the customer.

—Meg Barra
CEO, General Motors

What is the one people problem I least want to address?

In the end, it is important to remember that we cannot become what we need to be by remaining what we are.

—Max De Pree
Businessman & Writer

What do I want in my obituary?

Life's value is not its duration but its donation—not how long we live, but how fully and how well.

—J. Oswald Sanders
Author

What would I do differently if I started over from scratch?

Today I will do what others won't, so tomorrow I can accomplish what others can't.

—Jerry Rice
Professional Football Player

What is our value proposition and what should I do to strengthen it?

If you are not willing to risk the usual, you will have to settle for the ordinary.

—Jim Rohn
Author & Speaker

What fulfills me?

There is no passion to be found playing small—in settling for a life that is less than the one you are capable of living.

—Nelson Mandela

What do I want?

Speak your truth, even if your voice shakes.

—Robin Sharma
Writer

Why do I want what I want?

You have to do something in your life that is honorable and not cowardly if you are to live in peace with yourself.

—Larry Brown
Professional Basketball Coach

What do I fear being asked?

Fear keeps us focused on the past or worried about the future.

—Thich Nhat Hanh
Buddhist Monk

If I don't change anything, how will my business and my family turn out in five years? How about my interior life?

Knowing what I am to own and take responsibility for gives me freedom. Taking responsibility for my life opens up many different options.

—Dr. Henry Cloud
Psychologist & Author

Why am I still running this company?

People can have two different mindsets. Those with a "fixed mindset" believe that their talents and abilities are carved in stone. Those with a "growth mindset" believe that their talents and abilities can be developed. Fixed mindsets see every encounter as a test of their worthiness. Growth mindsets see the same encounters as opportunities to improve.

—Daniel H. Pink
Author & Speaker

What conversations would I have if I knew I was dying in one week?

Leadership is about making others better as a result of your presence and making sure that impact lasts in your absence.

—Sheryl Sandberg
COO, Facebook

What must I change to fulfill my calling for a long run?

Yesterday I was clever, so I wanted to change the world. Today I am wise, so I am changing myself.

—Rumi

What do I wish I knew?

You must continually increase your learning, the way you think, and the way you approach the organization. I've never forgotten that.

—Indra Nooyi
CEO, PepsiCo

Is there a way for my business to be ten times more successful?

You've got to look at the gap, where competitors in the market have grown lazy and lost contact.

—Rupert Murdoch
Founder, 21st Century Fox

How is the market changing, and what am I going to do about it?

I can be changed by what happens to me. But I refuse to be reduced by it.

—Maya Angelou
Author

What do I hear from the very center of my being?

Cherish your visions. Cherish your ideals. Cherish the music that stirs in your heart, the beauty that forms in your mind, the loveliness that drapes your purest thoughts.

For out of them will grow all delightful conditions, all heavenly environment, of these, if you but remain true to them, your world will at last be built.

—James Allen
Philosopher

How have I given people reason to mistrust me?

Trust has never been lower in our world. The leaders who can bridge the trust gaps in their life and business, through human connection, are the ones who will own every room.

—Lieutenant Colonel (Retired) Scott Mann
Green Beret & Founder of Rooftop Leadership

Where am I on my journey of getting what I want from the business?

Those who know that they are profound strive for clarity. Those who would like to seem profound to the crowd strive for obscurity. For the crowd believes that if it cannot see to the bottom of something it must be profound. It is so timid and dislikes going into the water.

—Friedrich Nietzsche
Philosopher

Should I stay in the ______ business?

You have to be burning with an idea, or a problem, or a wrong that you want to right. If you're not passionate enough from the start, you'll never stick it out.

—Steve Jobs
Co-Founder, Apple Computers

What is the business's role in me achieving what I want?

Management has a lot to do with answers. Leadership is a function of questions. And the first question for a leader always is: "Who do we intend to be?" Not "What are we going to do?" but "Who do we intend to be?"

—Max De Pree
Businessman & Writer

What could I change for this business to make [more] money?

Companies rarely die from moving too fast, and they frequently die from moving too slowly.

—Reed Hastings
CEO, Netflix

What is most important for me to think about today?

Things which matter most must never be at the mercy of things which matter least.

—Goethe

What should I delegate?

When you delegate tasks, you create followers. When you delegate authority, you create leaders.

—Craig Groeschel
Pastor & Founder of Life Church

Am I giving all areas of my life appropriate energy?

Concentrate all your thoughts upon the work at hand. The sun's rays do not burn until brought to a focus.

—Alexander Graham Bell

What issues or struggles are keeping me from getting what I want from the business?

When we least expect it, life sets us a challenge to test our courage and willingness to change.

—Paulo Coelho
Author

In what ways is my business unable to grow beyond me? What should I do about that?

If you want to build a ship, don't drum up the men to gather wood, divide the work, and give orders. Instead, teach them to yearn for the vast and endless sea.

—Antoine de Saint-Exupéry
Writer

How could I change my perspective?

What we see depends mainly on what we look for.

—John Lubbock
Banker & Philanthropist

COLLECTIVE CLARITY

If you've come this far, there is a chance you've worn out the pages of this book—at least we hope you have. Think about it. In your hands, you are holding a year or more of moments when you moved from chaos to clarity by giving yourself the space to sit in your thoughts and lean into these seasons. Congratulations. You have accomplished something few business leaders make room to discover in themselves. But there is one more thing you need to know before you keep moving forward.

There is a fifth season, the season of *collective clarity*. As you have probably discovered through this process, not all questions are meant to be answered alone. There are people in your life who can sharpen the view for you, and those key voices should have a place in this season. Now, don't get us wrong. The incubator you create for your thoughts in these clarity sessions is crucial to the development of your wisdom and insight *before* you go to your team to hash out the details. Once you have done the outstanding work of creating personal clarity, the work becomes collaborative to move great ideas to great action. We have three recommendations as you go forward with the thoughts you have processed in this book.

1. START A CONVERSATION WITH YOUR SENIOR LEADERSHIP TEAM.

These should be the most trusted business leaders in your organization. Regardless of how your company is structured, these individuals need to be capable of pushing back, offer meaningful additions to your thoughts, and be staunch champions of the success of the business. But you know as well as we do, it's harder than it sounds to create ongoing clarity and control with your team—even with the best leaders in the room. Having a framework to guide you will give you a pathway forward to maximize your results and multiply the impact of the clarity you've found here.

Learn more about the System and Soul Framework™ at systemandsoul.com

2. GET A COACH.

Having the right coach to lay the groundwork for healthy conversations can be a game-changer.

This person should be someone who understands your goals and is interested in helping you discover the answers and empowering the outcomrd, not dictating solutions to you.

Find a Coach at systemandsoul.com/coach

3. KEEP YOUR EAR TO THE GROUND.

Some of your best insights will happen in the most random ways like hearing a solid one-liner in a podcast or finding your thought contained perfectly in a single sentence in an article. We encourage you to keep your ear to the ground. Listen for wisdom in all the free content that's out there. Brilliance is available to you all over the internet. But to get you started, we have a few recommendations for you.

System & Soul Podcast
A podcast to help entrepreneurs gain clarity and control.
Hosted by Chris White and Benj Miller
systemandsoul.com/podcast

Dr. Benjamin Hardy
Organizational Psychologist and Best Selling Author
benjaminhardy.com

Exceptional Leaders
Be the kind of leader others want to follow.
exceptionalleaders.com

Rooftop Leadership & Scott Mann
Empowering leaders for purposeful impact.

rooftopleadership.com

We trust this process has been remarkably insightful for you. And we would love to hear your stories. Follow us on social media or visit us at ClarityFieldGuide.com for more ways to connect.

We are both loyal to the tribe of leaders who relentlessly seek clarity for themselves and their organizations. If we can serve you as you go forward, don't hesitate to reach out.

Best to you in the journey ahead,
Benj and Chris

ABOUT THE AUTHORS

Authenticity, breaking the rules, and creating clarity are the core of Benj Miller's life and work.

He's founded ten businesses in his eighteen years of entrepreneurial experience. He's driven by the desire to help small businesses make the greatest possible impact on the communities they serve. He now dedicates his time to helping other business owners catalyze growth through the System & Soul Framework™ and find game-changing breakthroughs in the process. As an advocate for all businesses running on System & Soul™, Benj also co-hosts the System & Soul podcast with Chris White and co-founded the S2 Sync app. He lives in Atlanta, GA with his wife of twenty-two years and their four amazing kids.

Connect at BenjMiller.com

As a third generation entrepreneur, Chris White grew up with a strong sense of vision and drive to build businesses with great impact. In his twenty-five plus years of business experience, Chris successfully built four companies, but says his journey took a massive turning point when, at forty four, he discovered his unique ability as a business coach.

He now passionately pursues radically candid conversations with a relentless drive to mastery (and plenty of fun along the way) as he coaches his clients through the System & Soul Framework™.

As a System & Soul Coach, Chris has helped hundreds of companies gain skills that transform their businesses and now coaches other S2 Coaches on their own path to mastery. Outside of his coaching practice, he co-founded S2 Sync, an app for companies running on System & Soul™ and co-hosts the System & Soul Podcast. Chris lives in Orlando, FL with his wonderful wife Darlene.

Connect at CoachChris.io